AF480030

CONTENT

Welcome to the most iconic and stunning place located Arizona, United States - The Monument Valley!
Monument Valley boasts its iconic sandstone formations – the towering buttes and mesas – shaped by millions of years of erosion.

Monument Valley Park kinds just a bit piece of the semi-autonomous Navajo Nation, which is the most important Native American territory in the US.
Some say this place is one of the most photographed place in the whole world, it has featured in many f amous movies!

Next stop an well know building with the name of The Space Needle, located in Seattle, It is more than 180 meter tall and it was built in 1962.
On top, there is an observation deck, there's a glass floor called "The Loupe." It's like walking on air and looking down to see the ground below.

The Space Needle is one of Seattle's most famous landmarks. It's like the city's special greeting to anyone who visits.
The Space Needle is designed to withstand wind speeds of 200 mph and an earthquake magnitude up to 9.1.

Next stop if most important building of United States nation where the president and his family lives - The White House located in Washington D.C.
The White House has 132 rooms, including 16 family-guest rooms, 3 kitchens, and 35 bathrooms!

Annually, the White House hosts the Easter Egg Roll, where children gather on the lawn to roll eggs and enjoy exciting activities.
This is the president's main office in the White House. It's called the Oval Office because it's shaped like an oval. It's a room where president gives all the speaches to the nation.

Next stop we arrived at the very well known and dedicated for 16th USA president - The Lincoln Monument located in Washington D.C.
The Lincoln Memorial has come to symbolize the ideals of unity, freedom, and equality in the United States.

Inside the Lincoln Memorial, there's a gigantic statue of Abraham Lincoln sitting in a chair. The statue is about 19 feet tall and 19 feet wide!
The Lincoln Memorial is one of the most visited landmarks in the United States. Thousands of people from all over the world visit it every year.

Next stop is close to the previous one is the Washington Monument located opposite the Lincoln Monument! It's dedicated to the first president of USA - George Washington!
This monument is the tallest stone structure in the world. It stands at a towering height of 555 feet and 5 inches (169 meters). It's like a giant pencil pointing up to the sky!

Builders used two different shades of white to build the Washington Monument, hence you can see two different shades as you go up this monument.
During building people place a hidden time capsule, This capsule was hidden away for more than 100 years! It was rediscovered during restoration work on the monument in 2019.

Next stop is world's famous leaning tower of Pisa, located in Italy. It was built more than 850 years ago. It tooks more than 200 years to built this tower.

This tower is very famous for it's tilt, it started to lean straight after it was finished building.
This tower is one of the most recognizable buildings in the world due to its unique tilt. Engineers were working very hard to stop this tilt and prevent the tower from collapsing.

Next stop is the famous red sqaure in Russia and the Saint Basil's Cathedral!
The Cathedral is known for its vibrant and colorful onion domes. There are nine domes in total, each featuring a different color and shape.

Today the Cathedral is primarily a tourist attraction and no longer functions as a regular church, it is now a museum where visitors can learn about its history and significance.
It was built over 500 years ago, and some say that this cathedral was built using no nails, which was very new to that time.

Next stop is one of the most famous landmarks in London, UK - the St. Paul's Cathedral! It was built around 350 years ago!
This cathedral has one of the largest domes in the world, due to it's unique contruction it has some magic sound properties!

Inside the cathedral, there are colorful stained glass windows that tell stories from the Bible. They are like beautiful picture books made of glass.

The cathedral survived a devastating event called the Great Fire of London in 1666. The fire burned down much of the city, but St. Paul's managed to survive.

Welcome to the one of many famous places in New York, USA - the Empire State Building! It was built in 1931 during the great depression.
Did you know that this building was completed in just one year and at the time of completion, it was the tallest building in the world for more than 40 years.

It also has one of the most visited observation decks in the city, where you can see all the New York!

Many famous people visited this building, it also has been used to film many famous movies throughout many years.

The next stop is another landmark in London, UK - The Tower of London. It was built over 920 years ago. This is a place where they are keeping the crown jewels which contains over 23000 gemstones.

The Yeomen Warders, often called "Beefeaters," are the ceremonial guardians of the Tower. They wear traditional Tudor-style uniforms and share interesting stories about the tower's history with visitors.
The Tower of London is one of the best-preserved examples of a medieval castle in the world, offering a glimpse into the architecture and life of that time.

Next stop is another well known landmark in UK, London - the Westminster Abbey. It was built over 900 years ago and is used for ceremonies today.
The Abbey has been the site of coronations for English and later British monarchs since 1066, when William the Conqueror was crowned.

Westminster Abbey houses the sole remaining Anglo-Saxon door in the country, from 1050, made from a single Hainault tree grown between 924 and 1030, as per tree-ring analysis.
The famous scientist Isaac Newton is buried in Westminster Abbey. His tomb can be found in the Scientist's Corner.

Our last stop is most significant and beautiful churches in Germany, The Dresden Frauenkirche!
This church was completely bombed during WW2, but it was completely rebuilt and opened again in 2005.

Visitors can climb to the top of the dome for a stunning panoramic view of Dresden. The statue of Martin King Luther which was placed outside the church survived the bombing and still stands as glorious and tall as ever.

ACKNOWLEDGMENT

As a creator of this book, I would like to say thank you to all the parents who are teaching their children about the world's history and well know landmarks. It is our privilege to be part of this learning journey where our younger generation is being inspired by the creations of our ancestors and the ability to see how amazing our mother nature is. This book is also a reminder to all the upcoming generations that we need to participate in saving our climate and making sure that all these marvelous places continue to exist for years to come.

This is the first part of the book series "Around the World in 80 Kids Stories". If you have any requests or suggestions for the upcoming series, please let us know by emailing: Readinnshell@gmail.com.

We would like to add more value to these books and make them more engaging for all the children.

THANK YOU